UNDERSTANDING YOU

# UNDERSTANDING EMPATHY

by Elizabeth Andrews

Cody Koala
An Imprint of Pop!
popbooksonline.com

abdobooks.com
Published by Pop!, a division of ABDO, PO Box 398166, Minneapolis, Minnesota 55439. 

Printed in the United States of America, North Mankato, Minnesota

052022
092022

THIS BOOK CONTAINS RECYCLED MATERIALS

Cover Photo: Shutterstock Images
Interior Photos: Shutterstock Images

Editor: Grace Hansen
Series Designer: Victoria Bates

Library of Congress Control Number: 2021951846

Publisher's Cataloging-in-Publication Data
Names: Andrews, Elizabeth, author.
Title: Understanding empathy / by Elizabeth Andrews
Description: Minneapolis, Minnesota : Pop, 2023 | Series: Understanding you | Includes online resources and index
Identifiers: ISBN 9781098242145 (lib. bdg.) | ISBN 9781098242848 (ebook)
Subjects: LCSH: Empathy--Juvenile literature. | Feelings--Juvenile literature. | Social interaction--Juvenile literature. | Interpersonal relations--Juvenile literature.
Classification: DDC 152.4--dc23

Hello! My name is

# Cody Koala

Pop open this book and you'll find QR codes like this one, loaded with information, so you can learn even more!

Scan this code* and others like it while you read, or visit the website below to make this book pop.
**popbooksonline.com/empathy**

*Scanning QR codes requires a web-enabled smart device with a QR code reader app and a camera.

# Table of Contents



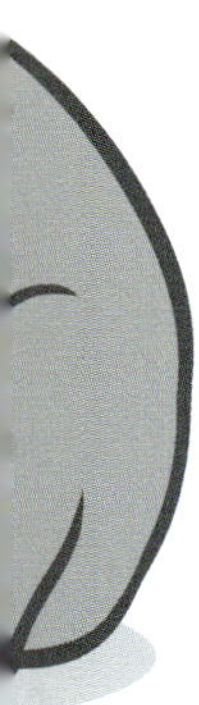

Chapter 1

# What Is Empathy?

Empathy is understanding how another person is thinking or feeling. Showing empathy can make you a better friend.

Watch a video here!

# EXCITED

- Moving a lot
- Speaking quickly
- Speaking loudly
- Red cheeks
- Smiling

# CONFUSED

- Wide-eyed
- Looking around
- Shrugging
- Pausing
- Asking questions

Having empathy takes work. You need to be **observant**. A person might not tell you how they feel in words. Paying attention to their **body language** and **tone** of voice can be helpful.

Observing people to see how they're feeling can also be called "reading people."

Chapter 2

# Friends With Empathy

Empathy is about sharing emotions. You can feel another person's feelings even if you are not in the same **situation**.

You can have empathy for animals too!

Learn more here!

Mary's friend Chloe got a new bike for her birthday. Chloe is very excited. Mary feels excited too. She knows how happy the bike makes her friend.

Tom's older brother Andre lost his championship baseball game. The whole family is feeling sad about the result. They knew how important winning the game was to Andre.

Chapter 3

# Understanding People

Another part of empathy is being able to imagine why a person is feeling a certain way. This kind of empathy is often explained as "putting yourself in someone else's shoes."

Explore links here!

Milo's cat ran away from home. An empathetic friend would take time to imagine how they might feel if their own pet ran away. Most people would feel worried and sad.

Milo's **considerate** friends decide to help him search the neighborhood for his cat. They offer lots of words of **encouragement**. They keep Milo calm while searching. Together they find his cat!

Chapter 4

# Offering Support

Having empathy makes you a good member of your community. Knowing how people feel or trying to understand why they feel that way means you can offer support when it's needed.

You have to practice treating people with empathy.

Complete an activity here!

# Making Connections

## Text-to-Self

What are some ways you like to support your friends?

## Text-to-Text

Have you read any other books that help you understand people better? Did you learn anything new?

## Text-to-World

Do you think it is important for people to have empathy? Please explain your answer.

# Glossary

**body language** – gestures or movements that can communicate how a person is feeling.

**considerate** – thoughtful of the feelings and needs of others.

**encouragement** – the act of giving hope.

**observant** – watching carefully.

**situation** – the way in which something is.

**tone** – the sound of words as they show a feeling.

# Index



Online Resources

**popbooksonline.com**

Thanks for reading this Cody Koala book!

Scan this code* and others like it in this book, or visit the website below to make this book pop!

**popbooksonline.com/empathy**

*Scanning QR codes requires a web-enabled smart device with a QR code reader app and a camera.